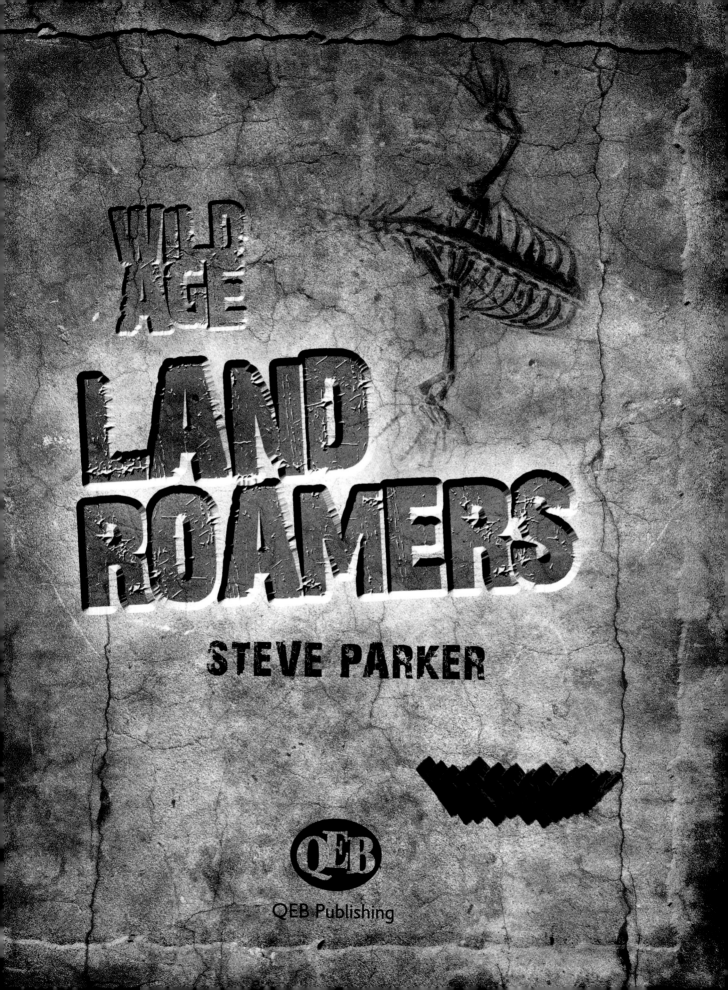

WILD AGE

LAND ROAMERS

STEVE PARKER

QEB

QEB Publishing

Project Editor: Carey Scott
Designer: Stefan Morris Design
Illustrations: The Art Agency and
    MW Digital Graphics

Picture Researcher: Maria Joannou

Library of Congress Cataloging-in-Publication Data
Parker, Steve, 1952-
Land roamers / Steve Parker.
    p. cm. -- (QEB wild age)
Includes index.
ISBN 978-1-59566-913-1 (lib. bdg.)
1. Paleontology--Paleozoic--Juvenile literature. 2. Paleontology--
Mesozoic--Juvenile literature. 3. Animals, Fossil--Juvenile literature. I. Title.
QE725.P368 2011

566--dc22

2010001153

Printed in China

Copyright © QEB Publishing,
Inc. 2010

Published in the United States
by
QEB Publishing, Inc.
3 Wrigley, Suite A
Irvine, CA 92618

www.qed-publishing.co.uk

Picture credits

Key: t=top, b=bottom, r=right, l=left, c=centre **Alamy Images** Pat Canova 23r, 30br; **Corbis** DK Limited
4cl, Michael & Patricia Fogden 5tr, Peter Foley/EPA 5cc (early mammal), Jonathan Blair 9b, 28bl; **DK
Images** Joanne Cowne 4cr, Peter Visscher 4br, 10-11t, 28cl (ichthyostega), 28cr (diadectes), Jon Hughes/
Bedrock Studios 5cl, 16-17, 29tl, Jon Hughes 5cc (giant land bird), 5bl, 15t, 29cr (desmatosuchus), Luis Rey
7t, 28tl, Bedrock Studios 24-25, 30cr (thylacosmilus); Getty Images Dorling Kindersley 12-13b, 13t, 28br,
29cl (scutosaurus); **Istockphoto** Dawn Hagan 3b, Breckeni 5br; **Photolibrary** De Agostini Editore 4bl,
4bc (plant), 4-5, 8-9, 18-19, 22-23, 27t, 28tr, 29bl, 30tl, 30cl (uintatherium), All Canada Photos/Stephen J
Krasemann 11b, 28cr (eryops); **Science Photo Library** Roger Harris 5cr, 26-27, 30cr (paraceratherium),
National Science Foundation 6-7, 28cl (tiktaalik), Christian Darkin 17t, 21t, 29cl (titanophoneus), 30cl
(hyaenodon), Jaime Chirinos 25t, 30bl, Laurie O'Keefe 29tr; **Shutterstock** Jim Barber 2t, 2b, 3t, 4bc
(cockroach); **Stock Exchange** 1; **The Art Agency** Myke Taylor 14-15b, 20-21b,
29br, 30tr; **Topham Picturepoint** 19t, 29cr (repenomamus)
All maps: **Mark Walker** MW Digital Graphic

The words in **bold** are
explained in the Glossary
on page 31.

CONTENTS

FIRST ON TO LAND

Long long ago, the first strange jelly-like creatures swam in the sea. Then came shelled animals and early fish. But the land was bare, with no life at all.

From about 460 million years ago, plants began to grow from the water's edge up onto the land. They spread and thrived. When the plants died, they rotted into the sand and mud, making the soil rich for bigger plants to grow.

Next, the first animals crawled from the water onto the land, to eat the plants. They were tiny **bugs** such as **insects** and **mites**, smaller than this 'o'.

Gradually land plants grew into the first trees. Land creatures became larger too. The giant millipede *Arthropleura* was as big as your bed!

First trees
385 mya

First reptiles
310 mya

Ediacaran	Cambrian	Ordovician	Silurian	Devonian	Carboniferous	Permian
		488–416 mya	440–410 mya	416–359 mya	359–299 mya	299–251 mya

550 mya   500 mya   400 mya   300 mya

460 mya 430 mya   360 mya

Shelled sea animals   Land plants   Tiny land animals   Shelled sea animals

◗ A creature now living, which looks like some of the early land animals, is the velvet worm. It lives in damp forests and is squishy and wriggly, but it also has lots of stumpy, bendy legs for walking.

● *Arthropleura* had a hard body-covering and more than 40 legs. It probably ate bits of plants and small creatures, such as worms and bugs.

Mammal-like reptiles appear

Early mammals

Biggest-ever land animals

Giant land birds

45 30 mya mya

mya **200 mya**

Triassic 251–200 mya	Jurassic 200–145 mya	Cretaceous 145–65 mya	Paleogene 65–23 mya	Neogene 23–2.6 mya	Quaternary 2.6 mya–now

200 mya **100 mya** **NOW**

230 mya **65 mya**

Early dinosaurs

Mass extinction kills off most land and many sea animals.

● Prehistoric time is divided into periods. Each period started and ended a certain number of millions of years ago (mya).

5

FINS TO LEGS

From about 380 million years ago, new kinds of creatures appeared. They began to poke their heads out of the water and wriggle toward the shore.

These animals were still fish. But they could breathe air using lungs, as well as breathe in water. They could also pull themselves along on land using their fins, which had strong muscles—almost like legs.

Tiktaalik was one of these strange four-legged fish. It probably lived in swamps, snapping up **prey** such as worms and smaller fish with its sharp teeth.

WILD!

Most fish have a head that merges straight into the body, without a neck. But *Tiktaalik* could bend its head on its body, making it the first fish with a neck!

HOW BIG?

Tiktaalik
8.2 feet (2.5 meters) long

◑ The fishy creature *Panderichthys* was 47 inches (120 centimeters) long. Its two front leg-like fins were bigger and stronger than the two back ones.

⬤ The fins of *Tiktaalik* had small, slim bones inside that were similar to the finger and toe bones of later creatures.

WILD FILE

Tiktaalik

GROUP Fish—**lobe-fins**

WHEN Devonian Period

FOOD Smaller water creatures

FOSSIL SITES North America, including Canada

⬤ Fossil sites

FIRST ON FOUR LEGS

Many land animals, from lizards to elephants, run around on four legs. But the first creatures with four legs didn't run at all.

Animals called **tetrapods** have a backbone inside the body and four legs. (Some have two arms and two legs, like … you!) The legs and toes of tetrapods were first used in water, perhaps for crawling through thick weeds. Only later did they become useful for moving on land.

Early tetrapods were *Ichthyostega* and *Acanthostega*. They could breathe air and waddle about on dry ground. The land was getting busier!

WILD FILE

Ichthyostega

GROUP Tetrapods

WHEN Late Devonian Period

FOOD Small animals

FOSSIL SITES Greenland

● Fossil sites

HOW BIG?

Ichthyostega
5 feet (1.5 meters) long

◗ *Ichthyostega* was halfway between a water creature and a land animal. It probably sunbathed to warm up, then dived into the water to hunt prey, like a giant slimy newt.

◗ This fossil skull (head bone) of *Acanthostega* shows its many small, sharp teeth. They were used to catch animal food such as fish and water bugs.

LAND INVASION

As four-legged animals spread over the land, they changed or evolved into many different kinds. One of the biggest and toughest was *Diadectes*.

We know how animals changed in the past from their fossils. These are remains of once-living things preserved in the rocks and turned to stone. Fossils show that *Diadectes* was large and heavy, with strong legs for running.

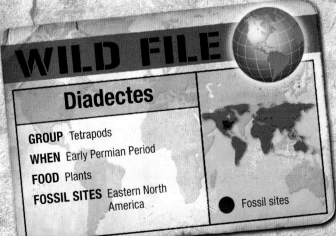

WILD FILE

Diadectes

GROUP Tetrapods

WHEN Early Permian Period

FOOD Plants

FOSSIL SITES Eastern North America

● Fossil sites

Diadectes had lots of teeth, but these were not sharp. The front teeth were like a rake for gathering leaves, which the wide back teeth chewed before swallowing.

◑ *Diadectes* was one of the first really big plant-eaters on land. It was also one of the first to hold its body off the ground on its strong legs.

◑ *Eryops* the tetrapod was 6.5 feet (2 meters) long. It had a very thick skull bone and strong legs for running. It could open its big mouth wide to grab many kinds of prey.

CLOSE COUSINS

Diadectes was a cousin of the living animals called **amphibians**. It was about three times heavier than today's largest amphibian, the Chinese giant salamander.

SUNNY SAILS

As more animals crowded onto the land, staying alive became difficult—especially when fearsome *Dimetrodon* was around!

Dimetrodon was one of the biggest animals of its time. Its long, sharp teeth are the sign of a fierce hunter. On its back was a tall flap of skin, like a ship's sail, held up by thin rods of bone.

Dimetrodon was probably **cold-blooded**, like all animals of its time. In the early morning its sail would soak up the sun's heat. So *Dimetrodon* would warm up quickly and be able to chase after colder, slower prey.

WILD!

In 1907 *Dimetrodon* fossils were put on display in New York. But they were mixed up with another large **sail-back**, the plant-eater *Edaphosaurus*—one of *Dimetrodon's* main victims!

HOW BIG?

Dimetrodon
11.5 feet (3.5 meters) long

◖ The plant-eater
Scutosaurus was as big as
a horse but much heavier.
It was protected from attack
by hard scale-like plates
called **scutes** in its skin.

◖ The legs of *Dimetrodon* were at the sides of its
body, rather than underneath, as in a dinosaur. So,
while the dinosaurs could walk in an upright way,
Dimetrodon walked with a waddle, like a **lizard**.

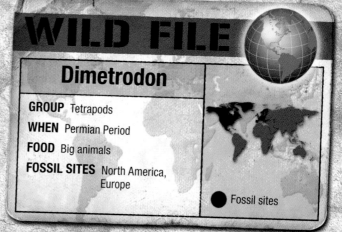

WILD FILE

Dimetrodon

GROUP Tetrapods

WHEN Permian Period

FOOD Big animals

FOSSIL SITES North America,
Europe

● Fossil sites

OPEN WIDE!

In 2001, fossils of the biggest-ever crocodile were found in the Sahara. What was it doing in the world's largest desert?

About 110 million years ago, in the **Age of the Dinosaurs**, the **Sahara** was very different. It was a region of tropical forests and woods with lots of rivers, lakes, and streams. Here lived *Sarcosuchus*—a giant crocodile as long as a bus, with a mouth the size of a doorway.

Sarcosuchus probably hunted in the water for fishes. It might also have come onto land to attack and eat baby dinosaurs.

WILD!

The biggest crocodile today is the saltwater croc. *Sarcosuchus* was twice as long and five times heavier. If *Sarcosuchus* was alive today, it could eat a 'saltie' for breakfast!

☻ *Sarcosuchus* might wait in the water for young dinosaurs and other animals to come and drink. Then, it would leap out and attack them.

WILD FILE

Sarcosuchus

GROUP Reptiles—crocodiles
WHEN Cretaceous Period
FOOD Medium-sized animals
FOSSIL SITES North Africa

● Fossil sites

● *Desmatosuchus* looked like a flesh-eating crocodile. But it was a different kind of creature called an **aetosaur**, and it fed on plants.

HUGE HORNS

As land creatures became more varied, some developed strange features. One of the weirdest-looking of them all was *Estemmenosuchus*.

Estemmenosuchus was the size of today's rhinoceros, with massive, powerful muscles in its legs and chest. It had a big mouth and sharp teeth. Its huge head horns were not long and sharp, but made of flat parts sticking out at odd angles.

WILD FILE

Estemmenosuchus

GROUP Tetrapods – therapsids, or mammal-like reptiles

WHEN Permian Period

FOOD Not known. Plants, animals or perhaps both.

FOSSIL SITES Russia

● Fossil sites

● Fossils of the skin of *Estemmenosuchus* have no reptile-like scales, so it may have had hair, like a **mammal**. It belonged to an in-between group of animals called **mammal-like reptiles**.

◑ Almost 10 feet (3 meters) long, *Titanophoneus* was a slim, speedy meat-eater. Like *Estemmenosuchus* it belonged to the mammal-like reptile group of animals.

WILD!

A **herd** of *Estemmenosuchus* may have used their horns to fight each other at breeding time. Imagine the noise as their enormous heads banged and crashed together!

HOW BIG?

Estemmenosuchus
13 feet (4 meters) long

THE FIRST FURRY KILLERS

As well as mammal-like reptiles, there were also furry, warm-blooded creatures called mammals.

The first mammals probably developed from small mammal-like reptiles more than 200 million years ago. In the beginning, they were rat-sized, and they ate small creatures such as worms and bugs.

Gradually some mammals grew bigger, although none was larger than a big pet dog of today. Some of them could have eaten dinosaur eggs or even baby dinosaurs.

HOW BIG?

Cynognathus
3.3 feet (1 meter) long

WILD FILE

Cynognathus

GROUP Therapsids, or mammal-like reptiles

WHEN Early–Mid Triassic Period

FOOD Animal prey

FOSSIL SITES South America, South Africa, East Asia

● Fossil sites

◑ Fossils of *Repenomamus* discovered in China show that it was one of the largest mammals of its time — similar in size and shape to today's badger. It lived in the middle of the Age of the Dinosaurs, 130 million years ago.

◑ *Cynognathus* had strong jaws and sharp teeth, like a wolf. It probably hunted small prey and chewed the already-dead bodies of big animals.

DEADLY HUNTERS

The Age of the Dinosaurs ended 65 million years ago. The land was quiet for a time. Soon new kinds of animals appeared, such as the frightening bear-like *Sarkastodon*.

Sarkastodon looked like a combination of bear and dog. It had massively wide, strong teeth to chew meat and crush bones. It belonged to a group of predators called creodonts.

Other **creodonts** included the wolf-like *Hyaenodon*, and *Oxyaena*, which was similar to a large cat. Despite their size and power, all creodonts died out by about eight million years ago.

HOW BIG?

Sarkastodon
Length 9.8 feet (3 meters)

WILD FILE

Sarkastodon

GROUP Mammals – creodonts
WHEN Paleogene Period
FOOD Animals
FOSSIL SITES Central Asia

● Fossil sites

◗ Unlike a bear, *Sarkastodon* had a long tail. But like a bear, it walked on the flat parts or soles, of its feet. Probably it was a slow mover, not a fast runner.

◑ *Hyaenodon* had a long, thin snout with sharp teeth. Maybe it howled at night, like today's wolves and coyotes!

WILD!

Sarkastodon had plenty of big animals to hunt. Living at the same time and in the same region were rhinos and creatures called chalicotheres, which were cousins of today's horses.

TERROR BIRDS

After the dinosaurs, most of the big strong animals on land were mammals. Yet there were also great birds who could put up a good fight.

Gastornis was as tall as an ostrich, but much stronger and heavier. Its sharp beak had a hooked tip, like an eagle. Its legs were very powerful with pointed claws on the toes.

Gastornis was probably a fast-running **predator**. It chased after smaller animals, kicked and scratched them with its claws, then pecked them to death and tore them apart with its huge beak.

HOW BIG?

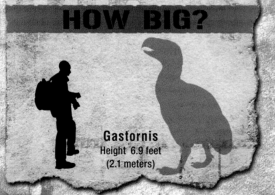

Gastornis
Height 6.9 feet
(2.1 meters)

❶ The wings of *Gastornis* were much too small and weak for flight. This **flightless bird** may have had soft, hair-like feathers rather than the broad, stiff feathers of flying birds.

Titanis was a fierce hunting bird that could not fly—like *Gastornis* but even bigger! Its fossils were found in North America and are about three million years old.

CLOSE COUSINS

Gastornis might have looked like a very strong, hook-beaked ostrich or an eagle with tiny wings. But its nearest relatives today are barnyard ducks and geese.

SABER TEETH!

For animals that kill to eat, the best weapons are teeth. *Thylacosmilus* certainly had big teeth!

Thylacosmilus looked like a big cat, with sharp claws, but it was in a different animal group, the **marsupials**. Its long upper teeth were curved like the type of sword called a saber. With its mouth closed, these upper teeth fitted into flaps in the lower jaw for protection.

Thylacosmilus may have stabbed its victims to death with its saber teeth. Or it could have slashed at them to cause terrible flesh wounds, so they bled to death.

WILD FILE

Thylacosmilus

GROUP Mammals—marsupial-like
WHEN Neogene Period
FOOD Animal prey
FOSSIL SITES South America

● Fossil sites

◗ *Andrewsarchus* was a giant mammal predator more than 13 feet long (4 meters) and taller than a person. It lived about 40 million years ago.

CLOSE COUSINS

Thylacosmilus was related to marsupials, or pouched mammals, whose babies grow in the mother's pocket of skin. Its near cousins today are possums, wombats, koalas, and kangaroos!

HOW BIG?

Thylacosmilus
5 feet (1.5 meters) long

◗ *Thylacosmilus* would have leaped at its prey. With its huge claws ready to rip its victim's flesh, and its massive saber teeth bared, it would have been a terrifying sight.

BIGGEST EVER

Today's biggest land animal is the elephant. Millions of years ago, much bigger creatures roamed the world—including a giant hornless rhinoceros.

Paraceratherium was the largest-ever land animal, weighing up to 22 tons—four times heavier than an elephant. Like many other rhinos that lived long ago, it had no horn on its nose.

Paraceratherium's head was 25 feet (7.5 meters) above the ground—6.5 feet (2 meters) higher than a giraffe's. This vast beast was a gentle giant, munching leaves, twigs, and fruit from the treetops.

WILD!

Paraceratherium was so huge that it weighed more than some of the giant dinosaurs which lived 100 million years before it. But the dinosaurs were three times longer.

Another plant-eater, *Uintatherium* was about as big as the rhinoceros of today. It had a knobbly head and two tusks for fighting enemies. *Uintatherium* lived around 40 million years ago.

Paraceratherium had a very long, bendy upper lip and probably a long tongue too. So it could reach even higher into the branches to pull off leaves.

WILD FILE

Paraceratherium

GROUP Mammals – rhinos

WHEN Late Paleogene and Neogene Periods

FOOD Tree leaves and other plants

FOSSIL SITES East Europe, Asia

● Fossil sites

HOW BIG?

Paraceratherium
Up to 29.5 feet (9 meters) long

WILD GUIDE

Panderichthys

Pronunciation pan-dur-ich-this

Meaning Pander's fish

Group Fish—lobe-fins

Time Late Devonian, 380 mya

Length 3.9 ft (1.2 m)

Weight 33 lbs (15 kg)

Arthropleura

Pronunciation arth-roe-plur-a

Meaning Rib joint

Group Arthropods

Time Mid Carboniferous, 340–300 mya

Length 8.2 ft (2.5 m)

Weight 220 lbs (100 kg)

Tiktaalik

Pronunciation tick-taa-lick

Meaning Burbot fish

Group Fish—lobe-fins

Time Late Devonian, 375 mya

Length 8.2 ft (2.5 m)

Weight 165 lbs (75 kg)

Eryops

Pronunciation air-ee-ops

Meaning Long face

Group Tetrapods – amphibian-like

Time Early Permian, 295 mya

Length 6.5 ft (2 m)

Weight 176 lbs (80 kg)

Ichthyostega

Pronunciation ick-thee-oh-stay-ga

Meaning Fish roof

Group Tetrapods

Time Late Devonian, 365 mya

Length 5 ft (1.5 m)

Weight 55 lbs (25 kg)

Diadectes

Pronunciation die-ah-deck-teez

Meaning Royal swimmer

Group Tetrapods – amphibian-like

Time Early Permian, 280 mya

Length 9.8 ft (3 m)

Weight 330 lbs (150 kg)

Acanthostega

Pronunciation ack-an-tho-stay-ga

Meaning Spiky roof

Group Tetrapods

Time Late Devonian, 365 mya

Length 23.6 in (60 cm)

Weight 11 lbs (5 kg)

Dimetrodon

Pronunciation die-meet-row-don

Meaning Two measures of teeth

Group Tetrapods – pelycosaurs

Time Mid Permian, 275 mya

Length 11.5 ft (3.5 m)

Weight 330 lbs (150 kg)

WILD GUIDE

Estemmenosuchus

Pronunciation es-tem-en-oh-sook-us

Meaning Crowned crocodile

Group Mammal-like reptiles

Time Late Permian, 260 mya

Length 13 ft (4 m)

Weight 1764 lbs (800 kg)

Thrinaxodon

Pronunciation thrin-axe-owe-don

Meaning Three-pronged tooth

Group Mammal-like reptiles

Time Early Triassic, 245 mya

Length 15.8-20 in (40-50 cm)

Weight 6.6 lbs (3 kg)

Titanophoneus

Pronunciation tie-tan-oh-foe-nee-us

Meaning Giant killer

Group Mammal-like reptiles

Time Late Permian, 255 mya

Length 13 ft (4 m)

Weight 440 lbs (200 kg)

Desmatosuchus

Pronunciation dez-mat-oh-sook-us

Meaning Link crocodile

Group Reptiles—aetosaurs

Time Late Triassic, 210 mya

Length 16.4 ft (5 m)

Weight 882 lbs (400 kg)

Scutosaurus

Pronunciation scoot-oh-saw-rus

Meaning Shield reptile

Group Reptiles—anapsids

Time Late Permian, 252 mya

Length 8.2 ft (2.5 m)

Weight 1100 lbs (500 kg)

Repenomamus

Pronunciation rep-ee-no-marm-us

Meaning Reptile mammal

Group Mammals—triconodonts

Time Early Cretaceous, 130 mya

Length 3.6 ft (1.1 m)

Weight 33 lbs (15 kg)

Cynognathus

Pronunciation sigh-nog-nay-thus

Meaning Dog jaw

Group Mammal-like reptiles

Time Early Triassic, 240 mya

Length 3.3 ft (1 m)

Weight 66 lbs (30 kg)

Sarcosuchus

Pronunciation sark-oh-sook-us

Meaning Flesh crocodile

Group Reptiles— crocodiles

Time Mid Cretaceous, 110 mya

Length 39 ft (12 m)

Weight 8.8 tons

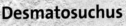

WILD GUIDE

Gastornis

Pronunciation
gass-torn-iss

Meaning Gaston's bird

Group Birds—flightless

Time Paleogene, 50 mya

Height 6.9 ft (2.1 m)

Weight 331 pounds

Sarkastodon

Pronunciation
sar-kass-toe-don

Meaning Protector tooth

Group Mammals—creodonts

Time Paleogene, 36 mya

Length 9.8 ft (3 m)

Weight 1.1 tons

Hyaenodon

Pronunciation
high-een-oh-don

Meaning Hyaena tooth

Group Mammals—creodonts

Time Paleogene–Neogene, 40–20 mya

Length 9.8 ft (9 m)

Weight 440 lbs (200 kg)

Paraceratherium

Pronunciation
para-seer-ah-theer-ee-um

Meaning Next to horn beast

Group Mammals—rhinos

Time Late Paleogene, Early Neogene, from 33 mya

Length 29.5 ft (9 m)

Weight 22 tons

Uintatherium

Pronunciation win-ta-theer-ee-um

Meaning Uinta beast

Group Mammals—dinoceratans

Time Paleogene, 40 mya

Length 14.8 ft (4.5 m)

Weight 2.2 tons

Thylacosmilus

Pronunciation
thigh-la-cos-mile-us

Meaning Pouch sword

Group Mammals—marsupial-like

Time Neogene, 20 mya

Length 5 ft 1.5 m)

Weight 220 lbs (100 kg)

Andrewsarchus

Pronunciation
an-drew-sark-us

Meaning Andrew's ruler

Group Mammals—mesonychid

Time Paleogene, 40 mya

Length 14.8 ft (4.5 m)

Weight 1543 lbs (700 kg)

Titanis

Pronunciation
tie-tan-iss

Meaning Giant, titan

Group Birds—flightless

Time Late Neogene and Early Quaternary, 5–2 mya

Height 8.3 feet

Weight 375 lbs (170 kg)

GLOSSARY

Aetosaur A type of reptile that looked like a crocodile but ate plants, with strong protective scales and horns.

Age of the Dinosaurs The time when dinosaurs were the main large land animals, from about 230 to 65 million years ago.

Amphibian An animal that lays its eggs in water, but lives most of its life on land.

Bugs Many kinds of small scuttling creatures like insects, spiders, millipedes, and centipedes.

Cold-blooded A creature that cannot make body warmth inside itself, and so has a body temperature the same as its surroundings.

Creodonts Meat-eating animals similar to the cats, dogs, and hyenas of today, but which have all died out.

Evolve When living things change gradually over a long period of time.

Flightless birds Members of the bird group, with a beak, feathers, and wings, but whose wings are too small to let them take off and fly.

Herd A group of animals that stays together for most of the time, usually plant-eaters such as horses, elephants, or deer.

Insect A small animal with a hard body casing and six legs, and usually two or four pairs of wings.

Lizard A reptile with four limbs, a long tail, a round ear patch at the head's side, and overlapping scales.

Lobe-fin fish A fish with fins that have strong muscles in fleshy lumps or lobes at the base.

Mammal An animal that has hair or fur and produces milk for its babies.

Mammal-like reptiles Animals that were partly like reptiles, and also partly like mammals, with fur or hair and warm blood. They have all died out.

Marsupials Mammals that carry their newborn babies in a pouch in their bodies. *Thylacosmilus* was an early marsupial.

Mites Very small creatures with eight legs—they are close cousins of spiders.

Predator An animal that hunts and kills other creatures for food.

Prey A creature that is killed and eaten by another animal, the predator.

Reptile A scaly, usually cold-blooded animal, such as a lizard, snake, crocodile, turtle, or dinosaur.

Sahara The world's biggest desert, taking up most of the northern part of Africa. Once it was a wet area and home to giant crocodile *Sarcosuchus*.

Sail-back A creature with a tall flap or extension of skin on its back.

Scutes Hard parts, like big scales, in an animal's skin that help to protect it.

Tetrapods Animals with four legs, or four limbs—two arms and two legs.

INDEX